Contraband

Contraband

Juan Pablo Mobili

A Publication of The Poetry Box®

Editing, Book & Cover Design: Shawn Aveningo Sanders
Cover Image: Miquel Bruna
Author Photo: Buffy Cardoza

ISBN: 978-1-956285-06-2
Library of Congress Control Number: 2021922201
Printed in the United States of America.
Wholesale Distribution via Ingram.

Published by The Poetry Box®, April 2022
Portland, Oregon
ThePoetryBox.com

To my father, Jorge Enrique,
who shared his love and respect for language with me.
Among the many gifts he gave me,
poetry remains one of the dearest ones.

To my mother, María Esther,
who made sure I knew that what I had to say
was said without apologies.

To Madalasa, my wife,
my dearest friend,
my guide,
and my salvation.

Contents

Contraband   11

Maiden Voyage   12

Hiroshima Mon Amour   13

Hummingbird   14

Crocodile teeth   15

Tío Alberto   17

The Last Warm Tab   18

The Ring   19

Elijah   20

The Doe Led Her Fawn Under the Brush   21

Early Evening   22

Warm Breezes   23

Baseball Cards   24

This Body   25

Praise   26

The Girl in the Garden   27

Victoria   28

Prosciutto   29

Holding   30

They Thought They Were Angels   31

First Dance   32

Letter to My Body   33

The Virus   34

The Suits   35

Crows   37

God, My Father, and the Bombing
    of the Churches   38

The Wish   40

Losing Your Parents   41

The Great Wall of China   42

Summer Music   43

A Few Things I Never Told You   44

My Brother Behind the Mirror   46

My Grandfather's Ghost Does Not
    Forgive   47

A Poet's Luck   48

The Witness   49

Farewell   51

Meetings With My Father   52

What Wakes Me Up When It's This Dark   53

Acknowledgments   55

Praise for *Contraband*   57

About the Author   59

About The Poetry Box®   61

I am
a man crude as any,
gross of speech, intolerant,
stubborn, angry, full
of fits and furies.

—Wendell Berry

❧

Things reveal themselves passing away.

—William Butler Yeats

Contraband

I come from a place where everything was banned
whatever was made of red and billowed
and the words that could inspire solidarity

What was prohibited included *songs*
the length of hair skirts and sorrows
the extent to which a body may love another body
visiting countries more welcoming than ours
the study of psychology if Freud and Jung were taught
protesting injustice or high prices in the streets
and mothers walking silently in circles
hoping their daughters and their sons would be returned

When you live in places
where a deep breath
may someday be outlawed
learning to hide what you might think
is an imperative

you become savvy about carrying suitcases
with false bottoms and paying attention
to moon cycles before you load the truck
for the night-drive over the mountain

you must learn to master all sorts of contraband
neatly fold the newspaper you leave
between you and the stranger
sitting on the same bench of a certain park
or memorize the password that signals
it is safe to shake hands

you learn to master contraband
but nothing will be sadder
than a secret you cannot shout

Maiden Voyage

Thinking of writing a poem
about the Titanic
sinking in its first voyage
stabbed by ice
sharp like a dagger

suddenly I remember
a story an old friend told me
about driving his first new car
out of the dealership,
only to be smashed by a truck passing by

This is the point in the poem
when you have to decide
(most art comes down to that)

choose your story

sink with it like an ocean liner
risk the huge dent right from the start

Hiroshima Mon Amour

By the time I was old enough to notice
anything beyond whether my parents loved me,
the library ruled the longest wall
of our small apartment.

My father had originally drawn it on a napkin,
rows of shelves of different heights and the huge door,
framing the oil painting he finished the year
before my brother was born, from a still frame
from the movie *Hiroshima Mon Amour*.

On the canvas the man's hand
cupped the woman's face.

He looked at her, but she looked away.
Her grief glowed.

Long before he ever thought it appropriate to tell me
of the tragedies of Hiroshima and being in love,
the man and the woman on the painting
became part of my life.

It took years to realize that the day they dropped the bomb
the world defrauded itself, that couple, and my father,
whose silence grew larger than an atomic cloud.

Every time we moved from one small apartment to another
the couple came with us.

Now I regret I lost track of what happened to the painting
after my parents died. So much still to learn
about all four of them.

When I walk into a small room even today,
I wonder if she still looks away the way she used to,
and I cup my hand.

Hummingbird

The only picture of Ramakrishna I've ever seen
shows a saint skinny as a rail
legs fine as stems, crossed
upon a mat, and thin arms
falling like mist upon his thighs

I am moved by that

I am still and always a boy from Argentina
who sipped the wine of his father's profound soul
and sucked eagerly the milk of his mother's godly determination

I could have been a body violated and alone
but I was not, and
I am profoundly grateful for that

I aspire to nothing less
than the courage of a hummingbird

flying in place
a hero to flowers

Crocodile Teeth

are not that big, really,
if you compare them to Godzilla's
or the Empire State Building,
but they are dangerous

I heard a man say once
its jaws could break a man's leg
with one half-assed bite
(as he hopped back to his canoe)

but unlike some aspiring Japanese actor
stomping around miniature buildings
inside a cheap dinosaur suit,
the croc's teeth are real

those teeth can punch holes in you
like my great-grandfather punched tickets
working for Argentina's railroad company
when it was still owned by the Brits

As far as I know, my great-grandfather
never bit anybody, either at home
or as he paced for ten straight hours
each car of a train that only traveled

one lonely length
from the Buenos Aires terminal
to a tiny station on some forsaken plains
day after day to be able to afford at least

one of his children an education
give one of the six at least a chance
to rise up and be a doctor
or aspire one day to go to Africa

[…]

and navigate a river full of wonders
standing up tall like the Empire State Building
at the boat's prow, ready to deal
with whatever lives under the water

someone who would not dress like a monster
someone who knew poverty's teeth punches holes

Tío Alberto

He was my father's uncle, really
but all of us got used to calling him *Tío*.
He had retired by the time I met him
but he had been a fireman;
he had risked his life most of his life
in a small town outside of Buenos Aires

What I remember most is his voice
because it was so rare to hear him speak,
and when he did, what he said would never cause
either injury or awe, so it was hard to remember;
still I'm convinced he was not shy but infinitely mindful
of what may leave or may enter when you open your door

He would stand, making unwavering eye contact
with whoever took their turn telling a story,
looking almost interested, and smile.
Other than his voice, it is his smile that I remember

the earnestness of his lips gradually forming it
the strength it must have taken
to bring the smile slowly to the surface
through leagues of dark ocean
angry seahorses
memories of fires.

The Last Warm Tab

My mom was lying in bed drinking a warm Tab
and having a cigarette, before the day even started.
                    —Sarah Woolley McMullin

She'd lie in her bed drinking the last warm Tab
before the day started and the '50s hit her like hail

She was born in a place her soul was never from
belly & root light-years apart
having the appropriate papers but feeling like a fraud

the car keys and small framed pictures of the kids
the only familiar skyline atop the dresser

How can we say anything's a surprise
when every day we crawl out of the same crater?
A prayer struggling through her lips

let me face you, world, after the last warm Tab
and one smoke
please
before the children start jumping

The Ring

~for my mother, María Esther

My mother used to tell us about a stolen ring

it was summer
at a public pool
at the end of an endless bus ride

my brother and I would follow her
into a wooden shack she called
the locker room and undress among women's
stares that made us feel like aliens

but the story said nothing of long distances
run-down bungalows
or the moss
establishing its capital at the bottom of the pool

The story would go on about the ring
how she left it on the bench
and how *that woman* took it but denied it

how the police did nothing
and the woman walked away
slowly
victorious
my mother's cheeks glistening with rage

My mother told us many,
many times, as if there was something
hidden in the story
that none of us ever deciphered
that someone at last might hear
and relieve her from retelling it

My mother carried trust like an obligation
like pale skin around her finger
like a ring.

Elijah

Rest in peace, Mr. Cummings

When someone decent dies,
the craters are deeper,
the moon turns darker,

nothing prepares us
for disenchantment,
tears are essential,
the chair creaks.

Of course, we know
how to crawl out
of every hole
in which we fell

but the hands are sore for days,
the knees bleed,

the hands hurt like hell
but they keep pointing up to the moon.

The Doe Led Her Fawn Under the Brush

The doe led her fawn under the brush
the moment she sensed my presence.
Her eyes stared at me softly but
her shoulders seemed to rally for reinforcements

and I felt misunderstood
picked on for no good reason
profiled
sadness that leaves no fingerprints

How could I explain that to the doe?
How could I convince a mother
she did not have to worry about her child?

After all, I could not recall a single time
that pleading to my mother to "be happy"
did not turn into a failure we hid under the brush

I could tell from the stillness in her eyes
that to her I was the enemy
and given the tragic history of deer
I had no chance.

Early Evening

Certain things never happen
in the morning when the gods
or the government can't hide

but in the early evening
when it's hard to make out faces

this is the time when mountains
begin to disappear and the way down
is treacherous
expected but abrupt
like a hero's fall from grace

Certain things only happen
when people find it difficult to see
but insist they can see clearly

Mountains know this

They can help
but no one asks.

Warm Breezes

I trust thunderstorms more than warm breezes;
there's something forthright about their roar.
I appreciate their honesty,
being warned of what's to come.

Summer breezes are a different story entirely;
they come with sphinx-like smiles
the type a dictator might offer you
a kind of "friendly" that precedes
a trip to the gallows, or a Ford Falcon
without plates parked outside your house,

lulling you to think it will be an ordinary day
until your best friend's aunt calls you
and, in a clear and secret code, tells you
your friend went out for a ride
with some people we never met before,

and that's when you wish you were a firefly
when dusk turns to full dark and your message
flickers unequivocally.

But what happened to my friend
happened when it was bright,
they came with their glass jars,
lids removed,
setting a perimeter around the yard.

When it was bright,
and the fireflies were speechless.

Baseball Cards

I cherish the one where Walt Whitman stops writing a poem
and plays catch with death at the edge of a battlefield

and the one of Lady Godiva riding her white steed on the outfield
after getting a pixie cut at the local village parlor

but my favorite is the one of my mother singing her heart out
while my aunt Nelly smiles at her sister and plays the piano.

My mother so happy wearing her top hat.

This Body

This body has held me
close to the world
for over sixty years
it has been a close
personal friend
to whatever in me
needed grounding

This body has been
a sacred elephant
that carried me on its shoulders
and also the ox ignored
up to its belly
in the apathy of rice paddies

If it weren't for this body
I would probably be
one of those clouds
puffy and unaware
of the possible honor
of raining one day over a field
that could go on
to feed hundreds

This body has been loyal
and it has also betrayed me
it has forced me to listen
and it has also resigned itself
to never housing
anyone wiser than me

Praise

~to Mada

I stood on the sidewalk outside the small airport
—cars humming as they waited for those who were flying back—
while my body received the warm wind as a forgotten gift

If the wind could taste like anything
it would taste like honey or a hint of honey
or even a faint leaf of mint at the bottom of a cup

Bodies are like dogs that every night sleep outside
and every morning are ecstatic
because they thought they'd never see you again

like the Mexican grandparents who blossom
into smiles when their granddaughter comes out
so happy in her white dress
with red roses the size of red roses

For all I know they have only been apart a day
but they receive her as one receives beauty
that very first time

like my body receives the warm wind
a blessing of dogs' souls that forget
that what they love
will be there the next day

like red roses
the size of red roses

The Girl in the Garden

~for my granddaughter, Sophia

She likes to find small stones
to carry

in the spring
when the bees stand atop
long stems of weed grass

she stops and gasps
the small stones still in her hand

I think she loves the garden because
she is the tallest creature there

Victoria

~to my grandmother and her victory

My grandmother belonged
to the tribe that wanted peace

My brother and I wanted war

we stalked the magnolia
hunted the lemon tree

The only thing that was abrupt about her
was her silence
a precipice from which
our loud talk jumped off
to its death

She knew that patience wins sieges
so she seeded green grapes
peeled them with her fingernails
cut them in halves
and set the bowl at the main gate

to appease the barbarians

Prosciutto

~for my father, Jorge Enrique

Food has a way
of bringing seasons
and faces
back from that place
before oblivion
where they wait to disappear
forever

Ripe melon arrives with my father
to my palate

My father sitting
at a summer table
the elegant work
of fork and knife
wrapping a thin
and precise slice of prosciutto
around each bite
of melon

Prosciutto
might seem a word
never destined for a poem
yet poems have a way
of gathering their flocks

the way memory gathers
the light of summer touching our faces
the sweetness of a fruit
the meticulous work
of my father's hands

Holding

Who would wat to be
the unemployed clothespin
the one with the resentful spring
and sad wood face!

I want to hold something,
keep it from falling to the ground,
root for it to dry,
feel like a proud mother
when I watch what I held
so dearly
safe in a basket,

knowing I had
at least a bit to do
with the way in which
someone will wear it,
sleep between two siblings
or loudly blow their nose
into its freshness,

to treat them with the love
you'd treat family members—
the ones you like, anyway.

They Thought They Were Angels

Those were the years when the Flying Panini Brothers
would soar onto the modest void of their small tent
holding a rose's stem between their teeth like a bear carries her cubs

As imperfect as they were, they thought they were angels;
on the ground they were fallible creatures, but in mid-air
they felt holy, like hummingbirds God made with His own hands

Those were the years when young women came back from the prom
with their brand-new dresses ripped under their coats
after some holy boy dropped them off at their homes

You could see them driving away, drunk and laughing
down the street, and disappear into a darkness that would last
forever in the young girls' hearts

Those were the years where all of God's voices led us to silence
to admire men because they seemed to glide under the circus tent,
unimpeached by conscience or society under their tiny capes

and now they are beginning to fall one at a time
like the fruit of a misshapen tree that finally dies
like impostors with wings who thought they were angels.

First Dance

I had a plan
don't be the first one to show up
don't smile too much
walk slowly back to where the boys were
hiding my wounds
from the innumerable rejections to come
and look as spontaneous as I could

but she said *yes*
and the slow song suddenly played

I remember my hands barely holding her waist
touching the cotton of her summer dress
my legs forgetting they had knees

but mostly my hands
the feel of her dress

Letter to My Body

I'm sorry I put you through so much
the way I renounced you
and the loneliness that replaced it
the smoking the lungs will caw about
the times you were defiled
and I said nothing.

But especially for that night
when *Claudio* was taken
in the unmarked green car,
hearing the steps down on the sidewalk
eight floors below,
the breeze ominous that summer,

how you vaulted out of bed
when a car stopped suddenly at the corner;
we became so quiet then.

Have I apologized enough
for all the times I went to sleep?

By morning the country
went from angel to monster
the smell of bread not to be trusted
our five senses under surveillance
the forty-year journey to New York,
its desert and its blooming
deserving their own poems

where you felt like a dog—
invisible because you are so familiar.

The Virus

At this particular time, on this ledge
where I stopped to catch my breath,
no tragedy comes without reminders.

This is not my first state of siege,
not even my first global emergency
if you still count the rest of the world.

My body remembers this kind of rustling
in the grass, the way it fidgets like a lamb
in a barn during a storm.

I know the taste, sour and steely,
of how things are likely to turn out,
people who did not need to die, will die,

some politician will get away with murder
some people will change their lives forever.
In the *Third World* we learned

how to *pick up the pieces*,
we know how to scatter the ashes,
some of us will only cry later, unprepared.

The rest can be repaired or, in time,
we will learn to live with it.

The Suits

Ray Conniff always played
as *Chito*, my uncle by marriage to my aunt,
unpacked the plastic Christmas tree
that opened like a giant beach umbrella
and hung each of the ornaments
in exactly the same place he had
each year before

All his suits came from a used-clothing store
that remained the fiercest secret in the family

Christmas Eve, as my aunt greeted their guests,
he'd appear in the living room in his latest acquisition
smiling—he was the only one I knew
who smiled that way

I don't believe there's a single photograph
in which his lips do not reveal themselves
the slight gap between his two top middle teeth
that my father had christened "the portal of joy"

My father could not stand him
yet he cherished a bargain wardrobe's beauty
and went on Saturdays with *Chito*
to the secret clothing store

These two men, who spent more time
at unexpressed odds than admitting
how much they had in common,
would spend the day together;
praised each other's purchases
and hid their bounty from their wives

I wondered then who the first owners of these suits were
how many tweeds and flannels hung from those racks
because their masters had passed away

[...]

how many were abandoned for a few pesos
by men down on their luck

I don't know what happened to those suits
after *Chito* and my dad died
I hope that whoever got to wear them
carried some of these men's dear and noble spirit

When Ray Conniff played and the plastic tree stood
my uncle entered at the high pitch of the strings
the portal of his teeth welcoming guests
like the manger welcomed the Three Kings

These two men, who had never liked each other,
would open their arms in mutual admiration
and compliment each other's elegance

and Ray Conniff basked in the zenith of his strings
and the Christmas tree swayed like a windy beach umbrella

and the ghosts of each one of their suits smiled
and tapped their bony fingers

Crows

My father, whose penance was a thorough memory and
a frail heart that broke like a branch falls on the silence of snow

My father had a crow that called him from the depths of its wing
pecking at every word he wrote

My father, whose education was remembrance
clawed upon the noble cortex of his brain

watched his mother dry the dishes
and learned too young to soothe her silence
with the tissue around his heart

Memory burned like a child's fever burns
throughout the parents' house
memory was a crow's wing
suffered feather by feather

yet each morning
my father cracked his shell
each morning he hatched out of his past
walked to the bathroom
shaved
and went to work
with the persistence of a crow.

God, My Father,
and the Bombing of the Churches

~to Jorge Enrique Mobili

My father was an atheist
he insisted on it
every time the conversation
drifted toward religion
or talk became about
driving my mother mad

My mother was the daughter of the devout
president of Our Lady of the Garden's
Alumni Association,
the convent school across the street

My grandmother was furious
her child fell in love
with someone who had forsaken Jesus
and would only offer my father a stare
as cold as the steel of Gabriel's sword

But the story is really about 1954
when our president decided
to empty every hangar in Buenos Aires
and bomb the churches of our city

The roaring of white light began early.
My grandmother, true to the Lord's mission,
walked to the convent and commanded
the nine resident nuns to take refuge
in the safety of her home
fifty feet from where they lived

My father, the thin man without a God,
was there and spent the night making them
laugh, pouring them *mate*, and tending
to nine frightened sisters
whenever he was not standing on the roof
cursing the bombers, daring their bombs,
a cigarette between his lips,
while they lit up the sky of Buenos Aires

The explosions went on all night but no bomb
ever fell close to the Lady of Our Garden

Then morning broke and the bombers fled
like vampires to the shelter of their coffins
and the nuns walked single file back to their convent,
led by my father, who insisted on seeing them to safety

That was also the moment my mother told me,
as she swayed in the memory of a triumph,
that my grandmother fell in love
with the only atheist she'd ever care to love

I know my father was given a medal by the nuns
it was gold-plated
with the Holy Mother's face on it

and although he never carried it
he saved it
just in case heaven existed.

The Wish

I dreamed my mother was alive and young again

Buenos Aires in the '50s
sitting at the beauty parlor
getting her hair done
talking, of course

It's Saturday
it's early
she's drying her nails
and she's happy

I remember
nodding at her
and that she smiled

I remember I only wished the best for her

Losing Your Parents

Their loss is always news
even if you've written
heartfelt elegies already.

Among the stones
Virginia Woolf packed in her pockets
I bet that two of them were
for her mother and her father
before she walked carefully
to the bottom of the world.

When your parents close their eyes
two moons eclipse your sun
and a distinct absence
begins to follow you

like a timid dog
at a certain distance
trying not to scare you
but keen on its mission
the way some animals
trace the scent of grief

or stones sink
the full depth of a river

or an orphan can tell an orphan
from across the room.

The Great Wall of China

~for my son, Sergio

My son sits with his back to me
and his disappointment facing the garden

He's mad and his back is beautiful
and wide like the Great Wall of China

I feel like a barbarian stopped on his horse's hooves
at the foot of the wall

kept away from its gift and yet in the presence
of its immense power

strangely so
like a father facing his son's back

Summer Music

the breeze this summer is more austerely rationed than wartime bread
thank God for the crickets' generosity, filling the stale air with music

July has been uncertain, filled with rumors of mortality, and August has
    not helped,
and my wife carries the worrying for our son like a shroud

the porch is a church tonight as we respect the dark and choose to light no
    candles;
we have been speaking without a single word as the sauce simmers
promising the solace of a meal prepared with volunteer tomatoes

and the music tonight comes from small creatures
scraping their legs on their bellies like guitars

A Few Things I Never Told You

You know I wrote many poems about you
and when I didn't, I was still thinking of you.

I said this many times to friends and strangers,
my father and I have been closer since he died.

I think people thought I was sarcastic, or clever,
or realized that some distance was needed,

that years must go by until you can see another man
for who he was, and even more to see your father,

with the eyes of a man who has traveled
equal lengths of grief and love.

Now I am almost as old as you were when you died.
Now you are someone I might meet in the bar

where you liked to sip on a vermouth and write
a few lines on one of those tiny paper napkins,

sentences that would not reveal themselves immediately,
although they were not obscure, because you spoke

exactly the same way when you told me I was too young
to go hitchhiking with my friends to a small-town beach

along the Atlantic Ocean; you said *when you*
understand the misery of the roads, you will know,

and I did not know whether that meant *yes* or *no*
but I went anyway, and you wished me well,

and to this day I wonder if you approved
or grew sad with my decision.

Come to think of it, it was the same when I left for New York,
except that this time turned out to be forty years

and we saw each other only once more before you died.
Such a long time to talk and we didn't,

we thought we would but we did not.
Now I only have your *visits* when I'm writing my poems.

We do get along better now when we meet
in that bar in Buenos Aires; we are both the same age,

share pictures of our boys,
confess we made mistakes,

and we take turns reciting lines from our napkins
like two strangers at a bar, hitting it off.

My Brother Behind the Mirror

~for my brother, Jorge Federico

What I failed to admit in me
I mistook for my brother
years were lost between us
great moments burned to ashes

To spend time with my brother
would unleash storms in my body
lacking clean water for weeks

My anger would linger
like a torn cable spitting sparks

Whether it was dumb-luck learning
or a sort of grace I doubt that I deserved
the storms have not returned
and now we sit together and talk
like brothers

the only citizens
of the country of our parents

and now the only thing that matters
is that I love this man
who reminds me of my mother and my father
who makes me laugh and cultivates
a kindness I don't speak fluently

who carries in his bottle the part of the message
torn from the one rolled up in mine

My Grandfather's Ghost Does Not Forgive

My grandfather was a boy when he got his first job
saving enough and joining the Young Men's Christian Association
to take the first warm shower of his life

He knew the bet on him was he'd never make it
but he aimed his whole being on proving them wrong

He wrote his master's thesis at twenty-one
became the youngest vice president of Otis Elevators
and helped to bring Chaplin's films to Argentina

but the scar of his beginnings never healed

he did not pray   he toiled
he did not hope   he persevered
he did not blame God, nor did he feel he had to praise Him
he watched from his one tower the arbitrariness of life

he loved, armored heart and all

but he never forgot that bet

A Poet's Luck

Luck knows nothing but this moment

—Sarah E. Gordon

The best kind is good luck
the kind that gives you
a break from being tormented,
and when they call your name
you are ready,
your paperwork in order;
your voice will touch someone

Good luck, you hope, will land on you
for being your best version of a good person,
although luck never decides
who should be lucky,
and some good people never are

But it's good luck
to take a full breath
and notice the breeze has made every bird sing
and for a moment being one of those birds

for a moment having a destiny
as clear as theirs

The Witness

Someone was knocking on my door
and when I opened it
I found myself dressed in a cheap suit
still in my twenties
holding a copy of *The Watchtower*.
Imagine my surprise!
I always fancied myself a semi-atheist
and here I was facing myself as a young man
driven, enthused with saving my soul.

The *young me* seemed startled too
but didn't quite recognize me,
he made a comment
about the similarity of our accents
but did not realize it was only the tip
of the proverbial iceberg
of how much we had in common.

Given that when either one of us spoke
it was always myself talking,
I did not interrupt him,
and I reserved my sarcasm for the next person
who might peddle at my door.
All I said was *no*. Just *no*.

Nothing about not being interested
or mentioning that he had caught me in the middle of an orgy
and he was welcome to join us, to frighten him
back to the van parked in the driveway.

I did not aim a single dart of cynicism at this kid.

He stood in front of me in silence
struck by what to do
with the gentle but firm response
of an older man who looked quite familiar.

[. . .]

He said "goodbye" and so did I
but added a "good luck,"
which seemed to surprise him.

As the van pulled away the driver turned to him
and seemed to say something but the *young me* did not respond.
I wonder if it finally dawned on him that he had met himself

the way he actually turned out.

Farewell

My mother passed away in the back of a Buenos Aires taxi
—her friend thought she was sleeping—

My mother loved taxis.
On buses she was somber,
circumspect like a locksmith
attending to the groove that would unlock a single door

but in taxis she would come alive
they were a luxury she let herself enjoy
delighting in the traffic
counseling the driver
on joyous purpose;
in the back seat she would imagine
what ease of means might be

Had she not chosen to be ashes scattered where my father's were
the hearse would have been followed by a caravan of black and yellow cars
you would have seen old and young men
driving without passengers in mourning for my mother;
trucks would not impose their size and cut anyone off for a change
and the lights would turn green as they approached each corner

I think she would have loved to know
that they all came to pay respects
a line as long as a pedestrian's eye could see
bus drivers would suddenly stop making fare change
and bow their heads

At the eulogy the priest would raise his hands and slowly say,
"Farewell, beloved passenger.
May the scent of vinyl that always brought you joy
accompany you to heaven.

Farewell."

Meetings with My Father

My daddy presiding over the crab remains at the picnic table
                  —Elaine Dixon

I've seen my father more often since he passed
it's frequently in the morning
when I write and he peers over my verses
having a smoke

or when he taps my head lightly in a museum
to nudge me along to a more important painter

or when I find myself alone or lost or utterly bewildered
and, shrugging his shoulders, he seems to say
welcome to your existence

These days he does not write poems anymore
but he presides over the crab remains
that gave their lives for families like ours
to sit together at a picnic table

the way he gave his own life to language for his two sons
and the idea that decency really matters

What Wakes Me Up When It's This Dark

my bladder or my soul

the thought that cruelty may lie inside the heart next to devotion

the nagging realization that the world my sons inherited
will need more repairing than the one my father left me

the counting of dear friends who left us
or chose some form of silence to stay among us

wondering if birds would remain flying
if they thought at the same time that they could fly

considering the irony of traveling far from what was evil
and stumbling into its familiar face exactly where I live

the mane of a dictator dyed in colors that don't exist in nature
what lies beneath the mane
the creature itself

my soul more than my bladder
my sons more than my soul

my wife breathing next to me
my wife next to me

her breath

Acknowledgments

Grateful acknowledgment is made to the editors of the following journals where some of these poems first appeared, sometimes in different versions or with different titles:

River River Journal: "Crows" (Issue 3, Spring 2016) and "The Last Warm Tab" (Issue 5, Spring 2017)

The Poetry Distillery: "what wakes me up when it's this dark" (September 2019)

First Literary Review-East: "First Dance" (September 2019) and "Meetings with My Father" (November 2019)

Anti-Heroin Chic: "The Wish" and "They Thought They Were Angels" (February 2020)

Red Planet Magazine: "Maiden Voyage" (March 2020)

Spirit Fire Review: "Losing Your Parents," "Victoria," and "The Girl in the Garden" (May 2020)

Mason Street Review: "Contraband" (May 2020)

New Feathers Anthology: "Hiroshima Mon Amour" (May 2020)

Thimble Literary Magazine: "Summer Music" (May 2020)

Pensive Journal: "Holding" (June 2020)

Glint Literary Journal: "The Virus" (June 2020)

The American Journal of Poetry: "The Witness" (July 2020)

Champions of Justice Awards 2020 (International Human Rights Art Festival): "God, My Father, and the Bombing of the Churches" (September 2020)

Redheaded Stepchild: "Praise" (November 2020)

[...]

The Worcester Review: "Crocodile Teeth" (Issue 41, 2020)

Broadsided Press: "The Great Wall of China" (January 2021)

I would like to acknowledge several poets who offered to read these poems and provided me with insightful and encouraging comments. For this, I'd particularly like to thank Madalasa Mobili, Rebecca Watkins, Siwsan Gimprich, Caprice Garvin, Kim Noriega, and Maureen Alsop.

Last, but definitely not least, my gratitude goes to Cindy Hochman of 100 Proof Copyediting Services, who first edited this collection. Her wisdom, humor, and caring were essential to making this book what it is.

Praise for *Contraband*

At once intimate and broad in scope, *Contraband* deftly and poignantly bridges the political and the personal, and is, at its core, a lyrical and cutting exploration of the meeting place between human suffering and resilience. In the seam, breath is outlawed, men stand on rooftops cursing bombers as explosions fall across the land. But here there is also a grandmother falling in love. This in-between place is a world where warmth and tenderness feast at the same table as dictators.

—Caprice Garvin, poet and novelist

These poems are full of gorgeous and fresh imagery. Often, their extended metaphors are used to bring attention to and examine our everyday lives. In this examination they magnify the nuances of ordinary moments, showing the beauty and grief and, sometimes, uncertainty and confusion of life without ever forcing an answer. These poems are a testament to how the mundane is sacred.

—Rebecca Watkins, poet, author of *Sometimes in These Places*

Juan Pablo Mobili navigates the branches of image that reach toward and draw from memory without a false step. His worlds, his family, his perceptions all do a dance that is a wonder to get caught up in, and the delicacy of his words belies the power of their impact. There are very few poets whose work is so consistently thought-provoking and heartfelt.

—Siwsan Gimprich, poet

I was struck immediately by its humanism, its lyrical command born of precision and restraint. Whether he is writing about the death of his parents, or the secrets that move within us like a second body, his poems are quiet chronicles of our mysterious journeys as living creatures.

—Robert Hirschfield, poet and essayist,
author of *The Road to Canaan*

[. . .]

Juan Pablo Mobili has a rare depth of understanding that shines in everything he writes. He expresses feelings with an authenticity that sometimes will lead you to tears and at other times, a humor that will make you laugh out loud.

—Judy Emery, publisher and editor
of selections from the tape letters of Robert Lax (for publication)

About the Author

Juan Pablo Mobili was born in Buenos Aires, Argentina, and is an adopted son of the City of New York. The son of a teacher and a poet, his work tells the story of the joys and tragedies of a citizen of two countries, willing to face life head on.

His poems have appeared in *The Worcester Review, The American Journal of Poetry, Mason Street Review, The Red Wheelbarrow Review, The Banyan Review, First Literary Review-East, New Feathers Anthology,* and *Spirit Fire Review,* among many others.

In addition to that, one of his poems received Honorable Mention by the International Human Rights Art Festival for the *Creators Justice Awards 2020,* while others have been nominated for the Pushcart Prize and the *Best of the Net Anthology.*

He has also co-written a chapbook of poems in collaboration with Madalasa Mobili, titled *Three Unknown Poets,* which was published by Seranam Press.

If there's a thread to his poems, is his lifelong intention to have poetry make the world a more hospitable place.

About The Poetry Box

The Poetry Box® is a boutique publishing company in Portland, Oregon, which provides a platform for both established and emerging poets to share their words with the world through beautiful printed books and chapbooks.

Feel free to visit the online bookstore (thePoetryBox.com), where you'll find more titles including:

Nothing More to Lose by Carolyn Martin

World Gone Zoom by David Belmont

Protection by Michelle Lerner

Songs from the Back-in-the-Back by Marcia B. Loughran

A Shape of Sky by Cathy Cain

A Long, Wide Stretch of Calm by Melanie Green

Moroccan Holiday by Lauren Tivey

Erasures of My Coming Out (Letter) by Mary Warren Foulk

Of the Forest by Linda Ferguson

Let's Hear It for the Horses by Tricia Knoll

Sophia & Mister Walter Whitman by Penelope Scambly Schott

What We Bring Home by Susan Coultrap-McQuin

Bayna Bayna: In-Between by Zeinna Azzam

The Day of My First Driving Lesson by Tiel Aisha Ansari

and more . . .